Fire Safety

BY SUSAN KESSELRING　　childsworld.com　　ILLUSTRATED BY DAN McGEEHAN

Published by The Child's World®
800-599-READ • childsworld.com

Copyright © 2025 by The Child's World®
All rights reserved. No part of this book may be reproduced or utilized in any form or by any means without written permission from the publisher.

Photo Credit
© Rubberball: 22

ISBN Information
9781503893993 (Reinforced Library Binding)
9781503895065 (Portable Document Format)
9781503895881 (Online Multi-user eBook)
9781503896703 (Electronic Publication)

LCCN
2024942747

Printed in the United States of America

ABOUT THE AUTHOR
Susan Kesselring loves children, books, nature, and her family. She teaches K-1 students in a progressive charter school down a little country lane in Castle Rock, Minnesota. She is the mother of five daughters and lives in Apple Valley, Minnesota with her husband and a crazy springer spaniel named Lois Lane.

ABOUT THE ILLUSTRATOR
Dan McGeehan spent his younger years as an actor, author, playwright, and editor. Now he spends his days drawing, and he is much happier.

TABLE OF CONTENTS

CHAPTER ONE
Fire Is Useful . . . 4

CHAPTER TWO
Fire Detection . . . 10

CHAPTER THREE
What If There's a Fire? . . . 12

Fire Safety Rules . . . 20
Wonder More . . . 21
Visit Your Town's Fire Station . . . 22
Glossary . . . 23
Find Out More . . . 24
Index . . . 24

CHAPTER 1

Fire Is Useful

How many candles were on your last birthday cake? Do you love to snuggle by a cozy fire? How about roasting gooey marshmallows over a campfire?

Fire can be fun and useful. But, as you know, it can also be dangerous. That's why it's so important to learn how to stay safe with fire.

Hi! I'm Buzz B. Safe. Watch for me! I'll show you how to be safe with fire.

Staying a safe distance from fires keeps you from getting too hot.

A fireplace or a woodstove can warm you up on a cold winter day. Enjoy the fire, but always stand back a bit. Being too close could burn your skin. Or a stray **spark** could land on your clothes and start a fire.

Matches and lighters are adult tools. Let your parent or guardian light your birthday candles. If you see matches or **lighters** lying around, be a helper. Tell an adult right away.

Always let adults handle matches and lighters.

Electricity can cause fires, too. Only put plugs into a wall **socket**.

Some heaters can tip over. Always keep them on level floors.

Lamps and heaters can get hot! Store blankets and clothes away from them. These items can catch fire if they touch the hot parts for too long.

Cooking is fun! To play it safe, always have an adult with you in the kitchen. If using a pot, hold the handle while you stir. When you're done, turn the handle toward the back of the stove. If the handle sticks out over the front edge of the stove, it could get bumped. Hot liquid could spill on someone.

Make sure your clothes aren't too loose and you aren't wearing long jewelry. These things could touch the burner and catch on fire.

CHAPTER 2

Fire Detection

Smoke detectors can "smell" smoke before people do. Their alarms tell you a fire might be close by. You and your family have time to get outside safely.

Smoke detectors should be on every floor of your home. They should also be in or right outside bedrooms. Smoke detectors need to be placed high on walls—about 4 to 12 inches (10–30 cm) below the ceiling— or on the ceiling. This is because smoke rises.

Don't worry! You might not smell smoke if you are in a deep sleep. But the smoke detector will wake you up.

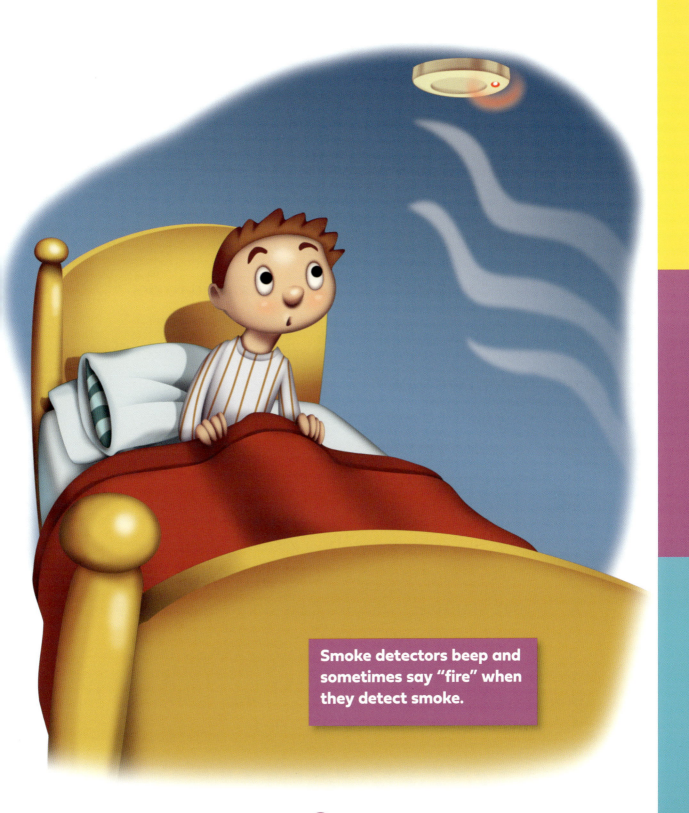

Smoke detectors beep and sometimes say "fire" when they detect smoke.

CHAPTER 3

What If There's a Fire?

Fire can move quickly—so you need to act quickly. Knowing what to do beforehand can save your life. With your family, make an escape plan. You should have two ways to get out of each room. Your first choice should be the door. Practice the plan until everyone knows it.

What do you do once you're outside? Go to your family's meeting place. It should be a bit away from the house. Some families meet by the mailbox or a tree. Practice meeting there.

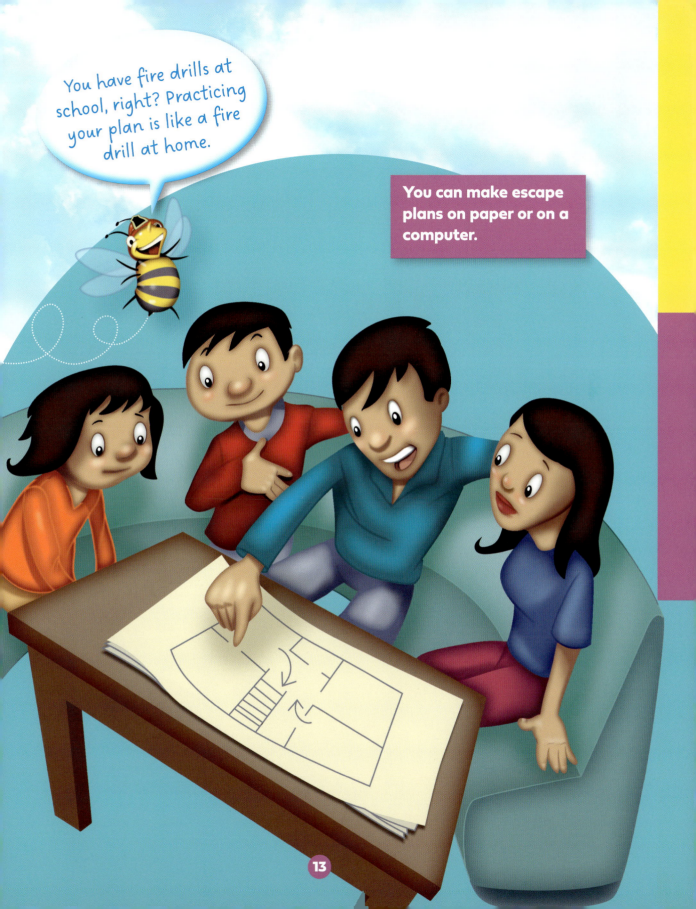

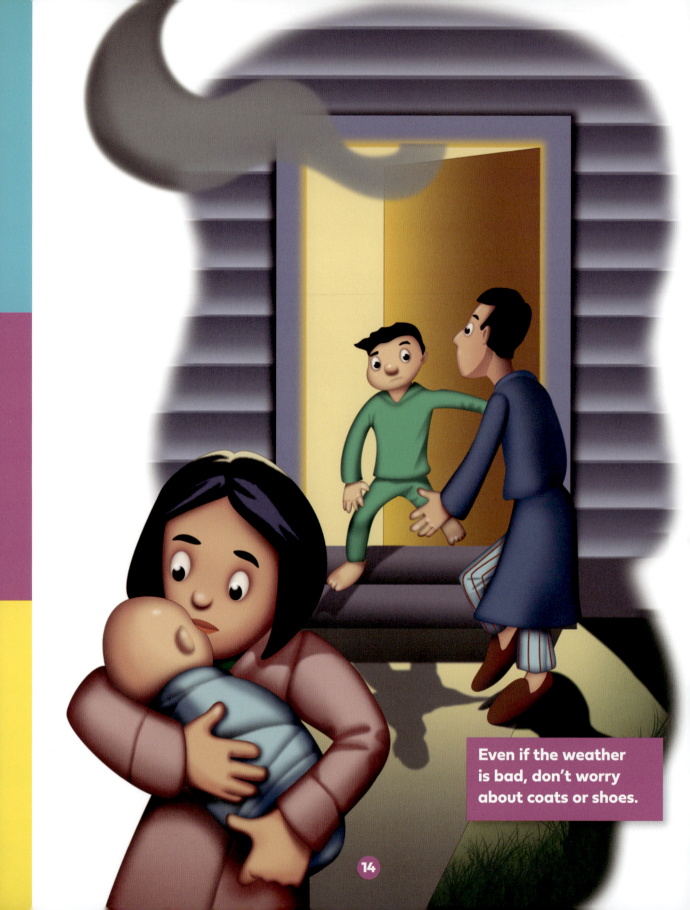

Even if the weather is bad, don't worry about coats or shoes.

If there is a fire, get out of your home as fast as you can. Don't worry about taking anything with you—not a coat or shoes or your favorite book. That wastes precious time.

If the smoke is thick, get low to the ground and crawl out. Smoke rises, so the best air will be down near the floor.

In a fire, remember to get low and go.

If you come to a closed door, carefully feel it with your hands. Start at the bottom and then go up. If it's hot, there may be fire on the other side. Keep the door closed. Find another way to get out.

Firefighters will come to rescue you if you are stuck inside. Don't hide under a bed or in a closet. Stay where they can see you.

A hot door can mean fire is on the other side. Check first!

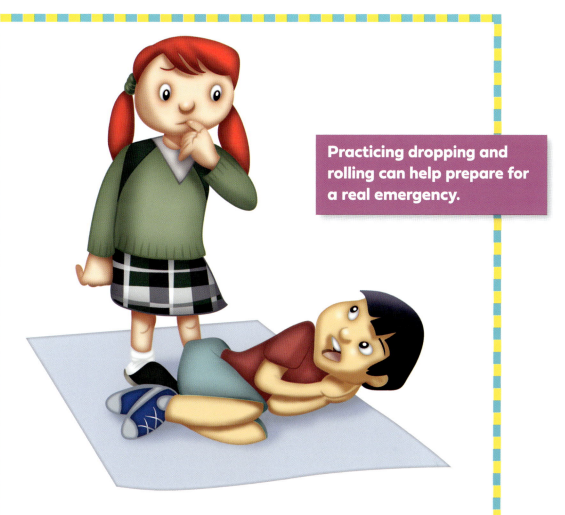

Practicing dropping and rolling can help prepare for a real emergency.

If your clothes catch on fire, stay calm. Running could make the fire bigger. Instead, stop, drop, and roll! Stop right where you are. Lie down. Cover your face with your hands. Then, roll back and forth until the fire is out.

Once you are out, stay outside. Going back inside your home is very dangerous. Fire moves quickly, and you could get trapped. No matter what, do not go back inside.

Call 911 on a neighbor's phone. Firefighters will come and put out the fire, and you and your family will be safe.

> Firefighters wear special clothes and air tanks to keep them safe in a fire. Do you think they look kind of scary? You don't need to be afraid of them. They are there to help you and your family.

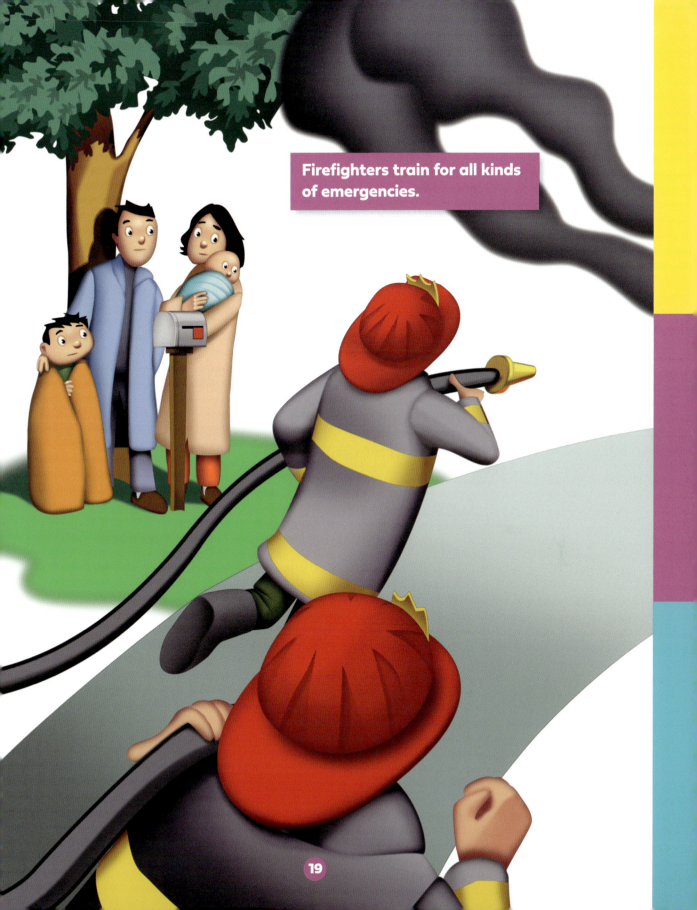

Fire Safety Rules

- Leave matches, lighters, and candles alone.
- Don't put anything over a lamp or a heater.
- Always have an adult help you if you are cooking.
- Have a plan for getting out of your home in case there is a fire. Practice it until you know it.
- In a fire, stay low to the ground and get out quickly.
- If your clothes catch fire, stop, drop, and roll.
- Never go back into a burning building.

Wonder More

Wondering about New Information

How much did you know about fire safety before you read this book? What new information did you learn? Write down three new facts that this book taught you. Was the new information surprising? Why or why not?

Wondering How It Matters

Do you know anyone who has had a fire in their home? Did they have a safety plan?

Wondering Why

Why do you think it's important to leave your house immediately if there is a fire? Why shouldn't you take your time to gather some belongings, your shoes, or other things?

Ways to Keep Wondering

After reading this book, what questions do you have about fire safety? What can you do to learn more about it?

Visit Your Town's Fire Station

Have your parents or an adult contact your local fire department and speak with the captain to line up a time that would be good to visit. Often fire departments have a special day for the town to tour the fire station. Sometimes schools have field trips to the fire department.

In addition to giving kids a tour of the station and the trucks, they will often have one firefighter demonstrate putting on, and then taking off the firefighting suit they wear when fighting a particularly nasty blaze. A firefighter in full gear with a breathing mask can look scary. But they're not really scary, and most fire departments love to have kids visit!

Glossary

lighters (LYT-urs): Lighters are tools used to start a fire. Only adults should use lighters.

smoke detectors (SMOHK di-TEK-turs): Smoke detectors are devices that make loud noises to tell you there is smoke. Smoke detectors can wake you up in time to escape from a fire.

socket (SOK-it): A socket is the place in the wall where you plug in electric cords. Do not put anything other than plugs in a socket.

spark (SPARK): A spark is a small piece of burning material. Stay back from a fire so a spark does not land on your clothes.

Find Out More

In the Library

Bak, Benjamin. *Firefighter Danny The Dog: Essential Fire Safety for Kids.* London, UK: WordSmith Publishers, 2023.

Dinmont Kerry. *Amanda's Fire Drill: A Book about Fire Safety.* Parker, CO: The Child's World, 2018.

Martin, Harry. *Fire Dog Bailey's Kid's Fire Safety Book.* Trenton, GA: BookLocker.com: 2017.

On the Web

Visit our Web site for links about fire safety:
childsworld.com/links

Note to Parents, Teachers, and Librarians: We routinely verify our Web links to make sure they are safe and active sites. So encourage your readers to check them out!

Index

911, 18
campfire, 4
candles, 4, 6
clothes, 5, 8, 17
cooking, 8
crawling, 15
doors, 12, 16
electricity, 7

escape plan, 12, 13
fire drills, 13
firefighters, 16, 18
fireplace, 5
heaters, 7
lamps, 7
lighters, 6
matches, 6

meeting place, 12
smoke detectors, 10, 11
smoke, 10, 15
sparks, 5
stop, drop, and roll, 17
stove, 8